Snowflakes

on Old Pines

Art Aeon

Art Aeon / *Snowflakes on Old Pines*
(Second Edition)*

ISBN 9781990060878

Publisher: AEON PRESS, Halifax, Nova Scotia, Canada

*The Second Edition is a republication of **Snowflakes on
Old Pines** (2006) by Art Aeon with minor revisions.

Books of Poetry by Art Aeon

Flowing with Seasons (2003)
Hymn to Shining Mountains: The Canadian Rockies (2004)
In the Range of Light: the Yosemite (2005)
Snowflakes on Old Pines (2006)
Prayer to Sea (2007)
Echoes from Times Past (2008)
Breathing in Dao [道] (2009)
The Final Day of Socrates (2010)
Beyond the Tragedies of Oedipus and Antigone (2011)
Dù Fǔ [杜 甫] *and a Pilgrim* (2012)
The Yosemite: Images and Echoes (2013)
Revealing Dream of Vergil (2014)
Homer and Odysseus (2017)
Hymn to the Canadian Rockies (2019)*
Flowing with Seasons (2020)*
Hymn to the Range of Light (2020)*
Hymn to Sea (2020)*
Tragic Comedies of Humans (2020)*
Virgil's Last Dream of Aeneas and Homer (2020)*
Du Fu [杜 甫] *with his Last Pilgrim* (2020)*
Following Homer's Odyssey (2020)*
Human Causes of the Trojan War (2020)*
Awakening to One's Conscience (2020)*
Hymns to Nature (2022)*
Dante's Sublime Poem of Light (2022)*
On the Nature of Humankind (2022)*
Cosmic Drama of Nature (2022)*
Tribute to Mentors and Friends (2023)*
Pilgrimage into Classics (2024)*
INNER VOICE {2000-2007} (2024)

*Distributed by Amazon.com KDP platform as printed books
and by Google Play Books.com as electronic books.

Prologue

Snowflakes on Old Pines
is a collection of simple songs
in the form of haiku.
They sing of nature
and appreciate classic
poetry and music.

List of Simple Songs

List of Simple Songs

List of Simple Songs

List of Simple Songs

{1}

Prologue

Writing in haiku—

Let heartfelt feelings inhere

in simple, terse songs.

{2}

Autumn Leaves

Colourful leaves weave

cryptic poems of nature

in profound silence.

{3}

Purgation

Snowflakes on old pines—

How gently they cleanse my soul

to breathe in pure peace.

{4}

Tranquillity

Calm, moonlit sea gleams

on still spring night. Bare gardens

await flowers to bloom.

{5}

Exuberance

Fine summer days shine.

Vibrant fields teem with lush life.

I roam through daydreams.

{6}

Rumination

Sitting on fallen

leaves, I muse. Inner autumn

pervades this meek soul.

{7}

Blessing

Snowflakes gently fall.

They clothe a poor wayfarer

on winter journey.

{8}

Spring Chill

Gloomy rainstorms pound the ground.

Tender buds struggle to sprout.

We bear harsh, cold spring.

{9}

Adoration

Graceful roses exude

fresh fragrances. I kneel to breathe

in blissful beauty.

{10}

Flow of Seasons

Fruitful autumn yields

to stark winter. I muse on

flows of ceaseless changes.

{11}

Empathy

Through drifting, dark clouds,

the pale moon peeks from stormy sky.

How I wish to soothe it.

{12}

Leisure

New, tender leaves sprout.

Tulips and magnolia bloom.

I doze in spring dreams.

{13}

Bliss

Serene sunset paints

sublime beauty on still sea

and peace on my mind.

{14}

Sowing

In deep, ripe autumn,

I prepare for blooms in spring.

With seasons, we flow.

{15}

Winter Chores

Swimming in my sweat,

I break ices to make footpaths.

Striving keeps us alive.

{16}

Voice of the Sea

Teach me, my sea, how

to grasp your numinous voice,

singing for this heart.

{17}

Art of Autumn

In vivid hues, lights,

and shades, autumn paints on earth

vibrant self-portrait.

{18}

Austere Beauty

Cold winter prevails.

Sheer steams arise from freezing sea.

It takes my breath away.

{19}

Capricious Spring

Mists waft on dreamy sea.

Drizzles awake new buds to sprout.

Fickle spring dithers.

{20}

Along Seacoasts

Whitecaps surge on sea.

Huge billows splash on rocky shores.

A man hikes in bliss.

{21}

The Last Rose

A withering rose

smiles in autumn. May it bloom

ever in my heart.

{22}

Winter Journey

Along frozen seashores,

a man wanders. Here, he seeks

warm inner haven.

{23}

Tilling

Spring breath wafts in air.

I till tough, barren gardens

to greet fertile spring.

{24}

The Sea and a Man

Vibrant sea inspires

vital spirit to a mute,

elated man to sing.

{25}

Winter Holidays

Our children come home.

The old hearth glows in warm love.

Fresh snowflakes heap up.

{26}

Wandering Freely

Balmy spring days lull me.

Let go of worries. Be free!

Take on unseen ways.

{27}

Quest

In calm, pristine dawn,

a man canoes at sea.   He

paddles into dreams.

{28}

Beyond the Sea

Bright autumn moon rises

on gleaming sea. A man muses

on the other realm.

{29}

Winter Gloom

Thick frosts glaze bleak lands.

Pale sun rises through sheer vapours.

Winter chills my veins.

{30}

In Mists

Dusk shrouds calm spring sea.

Sheer mists creep on shores. I stroll

rapt in reveries.

{31}

Vesper

Impressive sunset

suffuses vast sea. A hard day

closes in humble prayer.

{32}

Autumn's Poems

Reflective autumn

deepens in me. I admire

its pristine poems.

{33}

Daydreaming

Amid these harsh blizzards,

I dream of pure, fragrant roses

to bear winter's rages.

{34}

To the Sea

I come to you, sea,

to hear your deep, gentle song.

Inspire me to sing.

{35}

Yearning

Autumn touches my heart.

How could I sing what I feel

beyond empty words?

{36}

Desolation

Pale winter sun sets.

Gloomy dusk shrouds my husk. Despair

creeps in this sad mind.

{37}

Spring Thaw

Moon rises on calm sea.

Balmy breath of spring thaws my heart.

May it sing warm songs.

{38}

Ecstasy

Lush, fragrant roses bloom.

Colourful palette of lights

delights a meek heart.

{39}

Migrating Birds

Migrating birds fly

aloft across the vast sea. May they

come back safe next spring.

{40}

Winter Hike

Ice-glazed seascape gleams

in bright sunshine. A hiker

adores austere beauty.

{41}

Hard Time

Rainstorms thrash bleak lands.

Inner storms ravage sad hearts.

Anguishes rack poor brain.

{42}

Misgiving

Mists shroud unseen sea.

Qualms about myself cloud my mind.

How should I sail across life?

{43}

Doggerels

Paltry doggerels—

Why do I strive to write them?

To soothe this poor heart…

{44}

Summons

On vast, moonlit sea

of snow, a pensive man prays.

He invokes lost dreams.

{45}

Mute Heart

A fine spring day smiles.

Yet, my numb heart remains mute.

When would it sing again?

{46}

In English

Subtle foreign tongue—

How hard to grasp and lisp it

to say what I feel!

{47}

Recollection

Free clouds float in sky.

I stroll along pristine seashores

to bring back lost thoughts.

{48}

Plea

These curt doggerels—

May they gently soothe the heart

from which they've gushed forth.

{49}

Angst

Uneasy, sleepless night—

I sigh, watching crescent moon,

rising from dark sea.

{50}

Toil

Taut vicissitudes

of life—May I sing of them

in plain, heartfelt songs.

{51}

Autumn Glow

Colourful autumn

glows in splendours—Nature's pure

poems without words.

{52}

Ryokan (1758-1831)

Your earnest haikus

cleanse my mind as pure dewdrops

reflect Buddha-worlds.

{53}

Pause

Exhausted seagulls rest

on bare edges of frozen sea.

Life thrives on struggles.

{54}

Basho (1644-1694)

Soon, your haikus end.

Yet, they grow long and deeper,

tolling in my heart.

{55}

A Farmer-Poet

I till old gardens

to greet spring. I write new songs

to thaw this numb heart.

{56}

Yoon Seun Doe (1587-1671)

Like lofty, lone peak, you

rise above woes of worldly strife

to sing of nature.

{57}

Snowman

Snowflakes alight on me.

I wish I were a snowman

to relish pure snow.

{58}

Chung Huh (1520-1604)

Your terse Zen poems

awaken a meek soul to muse

on pure void in awe.

{59}

Snow-Buddha

Gentle snow-Buddha,

built by our beloved children,

sits in composure.

{60}

Du Fu (710-770)

Throes of dire miseries

you've sublimated in profound,

lofty, heartfelt poems.

{61}

On Frozen Lakes

Still, eerie beauty

of frozen lakes enchants me.

In wonder, I muse.

{62}

Li Bai (701-761)

Transcending this world,

your abstruse poems exalt

imaginative realms.

{63}

To Myself

Listen to nature.

Away from human's artful plays,

sing from your meek heart.

Snowflakes on Old Pines

{64}

Wang Wei (700-761)

Your sublime poems

inspire me to inhere in

boundless immanence.

{65}

Mother Earth

I toil on soils. Here,

I feel touch and smell of earth,

cleansing my dusty mind.

{66}

D'ao Yen Myong (366 - 427)

You sing of nature

in profound simplicity.

May I breathe in it.

{67}

Winter Sky

Hungry birds hover

over the frozen sea. How nobly

they fly in cold air.

{68}

Inner Chapters
of Zhuang Zi (369?-286? B.C.)

Fables of Zhuang Zi—

They seem plain, and yet so deep:

Abstruse yet cogent.

{69}

In Limbo

Listless throngs hurry

on bleak, dank streets in gloomy dusk.

A lone soul lingers.

{70}

The Odyssey of Homer

The more I peruse,

the deeper I marvel at

its cogent beauty.

{71}

Revelation

Elemental voice

of lively billows—How deeply

it pervades my heart.

{72}

Sophocles (496?-406? BCE)

Humans' sacred conscience—

How nobly it transcends fates

in your sublime plays!

{73}

Catharsis

Setting sun blazes clouds

on the vast sea. A meek man

prays in sublime glow.

{74}

Phaedo **of Plato** (427?-347? BCE)

Lofty, abstruse drama

on the soul—Philosophy

transfigured into art!

{76}

The Aeneid of **Virgil** (70-19 BCE)
[Book VI]

It sings profound mysteries

of souls through timeless journeys

beyond life and death.

{77}

Renaissance

Fervid feelings surge

with ardent zeal as if they

arise from my dead ashes.

{78}

To Dante (1265-1321)

Inspire me, Dante,

to pursue *Inner Journey*

deep into my soul.

{79}

The Angelus

Pale, ghostly sun sets.

Sea of ice extends to sky.

Meek man kneels in prayer.

{80}

Hamlet of Shakespeare (1564-1616)
[Mimesis of *'Mousetrap'*]

A play within a play

plotted by the player, inspired

by the ghost's saying —

How subtly Shakespeare plays all

in such astute acts of speech!

{81}

Trance

Snow adorns still woods.

I walk across stark, frozen lakes

rapt in blissful peace.

{82}

Paradise Lost
of Milton (1608-1674)

Despite his blindness,

how sublimely Milton leads us

to see his *inner light*!

{83}

In Haiku

Haiku's terse form forces

us to focus on a point

where things merge with mind.

{84}

Mass in b of Bach (1685-1750)
[*Qui tollis peccata mundi*]

Purge me from all sins

to breathe in this heartfelt music

for a rebirth of my soul.

{85}

Waves and Words

Billows sculpt stark rocks

along pristine seacoasts. I strive

to hew thoughts in words.

{86}

Requiem **of Mozart** (1756-91)
[*Lacrimosa*]

May I weep with you

to reach our *inner haven*

in your pure music.

{87}

Serenity

Mists sweep along seashores.

Dewdrops hang on rose petals.

A reed bows to breezes.

{88}

Missa Solemnis
of Beethoven (1770-1827)

Profound, cosmic creed

in music— it's too sublime,

yet so intimate…

{89}

A Heron and a Man

A heron poises still

on serene seashores. A man

muses in blissful trance.

{90}

The String Quintet **of Schubert** (1797-1828)

Deep, haunting *Adagio* —

What sublime, tragic beauty

it inspires in awe…

{91}

Reflection

A tiny dewdrop

on a frail leaf—How subtly

it reflects my soul.

{92}

To Beethoven (1770-1827)

You're so far on high

beyond my reach—Yet so close,

singing deep in me.

Inspire me to sing

what I love, trust, and revere

in pure, simple songs.

{93}

Offering

Snowflakes on Old Pines —

Let it melt deep in our hearts

to bring forth new songs.

{94}

Prayer

May I sing pure songs

to purge my soul and pray for

all humanity.